The Children's Mite
Promoting LOVE, CARE and CONCERN

EVANGELIST KING

Copyright © 2015 The Children's Mite. All rights reserved.

This book may not be copied or reprinted for commercial gain or profit. The use of short quotations, prayers or occasional page copying for personal or group bible study is permitted and encouraged.

Although every precaution has been taken to verify the accuracy of the information contained herein, the author and publisher assume no responsibility for any errors or omissions. No liability is assumed for damages that may result from the use of information contained within.

Scripture quotations are taken from the King James Version (KJV).

ISBN-13: 978-0692466551 (The Children's Mite)
ISBN-10: 069246655X

THE CHILDREN'S MITE

Giving to others is a way of showing concern and care, with humbleness of heart willing to bear. Being interested enough to ask if things are fine, showing love to all mankind.

The attitude of a child is that of having <u>no</u> doubts or fears, remembering the good with the bad, enduring for years. Every child, whether young or old, needs love, to love, and with it be bold.

Serving others with mercy and grace, being indifferent to the color of another ones face. Tolerance and obedience should always be taught; parents, guide your children so they can avoid being caught. Being frugal does not mean that you are cheap; remind yourself that some have no home, only the ground as a place to sleep.

Showing true emotions are not a sign of being weak, be as a child, show empathy when you speak. Give thanks for the little things in life, and remember those who, it seems, live in continuous strife.

—Roger D. King (1994)

CONTENTS

Acknowledgements	i
Preface	1
The Fetus Stage of *The Children's Mite*	2
The Birth of *The Children's Mite*	4
Mission	5
A-Maze-N-Penny	7
The Front Side	9
The Flip Side	10
God's Crayons of Love	14
God's Steps of Love	15
The 7 Steps to Color "Love"	17
Surrender to Reap Your Spiritual Inheritance	24
A Special Children's Activity	28
A Prayer Soldier's Story	29
The Whole Armor of God	37
Children's Stories	38
The Unselfish Family	38
The True King and I	39
The Little Boy Who Colored Love	41
The Coins of the Rich Man	43
Acts of Kindness: Should They Be Repaid? If So, By Whom?	45

Is Suicide "A Way-Out"? 48

An Open Letter to God 51
   The "Un-adorable" Child 51

The Conclusion 54
   The Seed 54

ACKNOWLEDGEMENTS

Firstly, I want to thank my Lord and Savior, Jesus Christ for His strength and loving mercy. Truly, if it was not for Him, I would have given up MANY times. I thank God the Father through Him for His Spirit Who is my Helper and Guidance. Secondly, I want to thank Mr. John Halford for his obedience to God. For it was through his article in which I read that God answered the cries of my heart.

Shalom †

PREFACE

As I watch daily how the people around me go about their repetitious and busy lives, I wonder, "What type of examples are we giving those little and fragile minds (our children)?" Do we, as adults, value to the greatest extent the little things in life? Ask yourself that question and, to your surprise, that is how our children feel. We are living in a selfish world. In a world where everyone cares about his or her own. Everyday our children are seeing examples of selfishness, whether on TV (i.e., commercials on how to buy games, toys, clothes for <u>them</u>) or at home (i.e., mommy <u>I</u> want this or daddy <u>I</u> want that). Children possess a special quality—all children. A quality that is so unique that Jesus Christ warned adults that unless we become as little children, we will by no means enter the kingdom of heaven. That special quality is humility.[1] But adults must teach and set examples of humility for their children throughout their continuous growth by giving, caring and sharing toward others; only then will the special quality within children never cease to exist; for it takes humility to

---

[1] Matthew 18:3-4

love God and others. For Jesus said, "We shall love the Lord with all our heart, soul and mind. This is the first and great commandment. And the second is like it, "We shall love our neighbor as our self."[2]

The Fetus Stage of *The Children's Mite*

I can remember some experiences as a child concerning a penny. I would wonder why I could never forget it and now I see why. God had a purpose. By not forgetting, it helped me to be considerate of others. My family was very poor. After the separation of my parents; my mother, who was only 19 years old, moved in with her mother and stepfather which made us to be a family of 11 children. Times were hard. We barely had enough food to eat. The family's income was less than $300 a month, but God provided what we needed in order to survive.

One day I remember having a penny and I looked at it and said, "What can I do with this?" I answered, "Nothing." So I threw it away. The next day we did not have anything to eat and I found a dime. In those days you had to pay 1¢ on a dime for tax. Our local store sold "two for a penny" cookies. I knew if I could get 20 cookies, it would conquer the hunger and would be my meal for that day, but I only had 10¢ and no penny for tax. As I stood there God brought back the thoughts of the previous day when I threw a penny away. I ran to the field where I had thrown it and looked diligently, but I never found it. In my heart, I was sorry for throwing the penny away. I missed my

---

[2] Matthew 22:37-39

blessing that day by not appreciating the little things in life by thinking (when I didn't need it) a penny had no value.

You see, it was pride and selfishness on my part. Because pride and selfishness said, "I did not need it." But humility would have said, "Pick the coin up and trust God for guidance." To be honest I never even noticed the written words on American coins, "IN GOD WE TRUST." My only concern was spending the money. I failed to trust God in believing that good things come to those that wait patiently on Him for guidance. I had put my trust directly on the coin in not believing the written words on them, "IN GOD WE TRUST". I only cared about my own desire and need. I felt that if I could not use the penny, then it was not needed. I was not concerned if someone else could have used it. Regardless of how rich or poor we are, it does not exclude us from giving, sharing, being loving, caring and concerned about others.

My next experience was more positive. Again I was very hungry, but this time I had a penny and nothing else. The local neighborhood store was about two or three blocks from our house. At the store, there was a gumball machine. It had small and large gumballs. The bigger gumballs were worth 5¢ and had specks on them. The kids called them speckled balls. I walked to the store and this time I believed in the written words on the coin. I trusted God in hopes of winning a speckled ball. I figured if I won a speckled ball, I could get five "two for a penny" cookies and it would be my meal for that day. I slowly approached the machine. I placed the coin in the slot and turned the knob and behold! I won a speckled ball! I was so happy that day. And I also knew it was God who answered my prayer in allowing me to win. For years and up until now, I

ALL WE'RE ASKING FOR IS "YOUR 2¢ WORTH."

know that Jesus lives and answer prayers!

The Birth of *The Children's Mite*

In the Nov./Dec., 1994 issue of The Plain Truth, editor John Halford wrote an article entitled, "The Challenge of Africa". In that article, Sister Mariola Mierzejewska, Superintendent of the Kasisi Orphanage in Zambia stated, "All I need is 12 Kwacha (about 2¢) and I can feed a child for a day." I could not stop from wondering, "Do children (and adults) in America value a penny?" How many times have pennies been stepped over, thrown away and ignored? Not knowing that we walked over, thrown and ignored God, because those pennies could have provided meals for homeless and starving children.[3] Because of Sister Mariola's comment, The Children's Mite was born. The word "mite" is Greek and means "a small piece of coin" which was considered to be of great value during its time. In today's society, it is looked on as being an insignificant and worthless amount of one's service. This is where the program begins.

---

[3] Matthew 25:41-45

MISSION

The Children's Mite Program teaches value to children (and adults) whether physical, moral, ethical, virtuous, or spiritual. This program is a way in which children can help to provide school feedings for impoverished children. Their "2¢ Worth" can accomplish this mission. Therefore, learning the true value of love, care, and concern. Some people think there is no need to show concern and care about the devastation in Africa, a continent where hundreds of thousands of children are dying daily from physical poverty (e.g., clean water, food, shelter, education), but we should. As you continue to read this book, you'll see why.

The Children's Mite is a 501(3)(c) non-profit, educational, charitable and Christian organization that serves as a tool in promoting the awareness of care and concern among children (and adults) towards the life and education of physically and spiritually impoverished children (and adults); with Africa being the initial focal point due to tremendous devastation.

Another aim of ours is to terminate the "middle-man." By mailing your own contributions directly, no administrative cost can be deducted from your contributions. This will enable the children to receive the full amount. Let's thank God for His wisdom and the understanding of His Word.

ALL WE'RE ASKING FOR IS "YOUR 2¢ WORTH."

We (The Children's Mite) operate strictly on donations, whether it's from our pockets or yours; so your donations are greatly appreciated.

If you are interested in this serving opportunity for children (and adults), please be sure to let us know and we will give you names of small and struggling ministries located in Africa that need and appreciates a child's "mite-sized" contribution.

This program is...
A way of keeping the special quality (humility) in our children from dying in a selfish world.
All about children giving their mites (coins) to the impoverished children of the world in order to provide food and education.

This program will...
direct children to be caring, concerned, and loving toward the welfare of others.
continue to remind children of the attitude of God which is necessary in order to cope with the pitfalls, peer pressures and failures in life.

THE CHILDREN'S MITE

A-Maze-N-Penny

Children from many schools in the Wayne County District of North Carolina participated in our program by saving their mites (i.e., pennies, nickels, dimes, and quarters) which totaled over $2,700 and was contributed directly to orphanages in Kenya. No middle-man was needed! The money was used to provide impoverished children with school meals.

This program will show how one can make a difference in someone's life. It doesn't matter if you are a child or an adult; because whether the coins are "from a child" or "for a child," they are still the children's mites.

Below are letters sent to us by two of our recipients:

Thank you very much for your letter and all the information about "The Children's Mite". It is a very beautiful idea which helps not only African children but also those in America who thanks to you are able to develop concerned attitude for our poor children in their

ALL WE'RE ASKING FOR IS "YOUR 2¢ WORTH."

hearts. May God bless you and reward you for this beautiful idea. I can assure you that we will be very grateful for any help you can offer us. We have 130 children in our orphanage at the moment and 35 of them are HIV positive. These children need special care and love because love sometimes helps them more than medicine. Thanks to you we will be able to give our children some extra food and everything they need in their daily life. Once again we thank you very much for everything you have done for us. Please, pray for us that God would help us to solve this problem. We pray for you and all the children of America. I hope you and your family are fine. With my kindest regards.

—Sister Mariola; Lusaka, Zambia

I have just received a copy of the newsletter Jan-Feb, 1999 issue. Thank you. I was very shocked and, I may add, angry also, that the wonderful work you are doing through Children's Mite program is being questioned and attacked in any way. It is such an honest and Christ-like way of helping children. In 1998, I have been able to send one thousand and thirty eight dollars to missions in Kenya from 10 different churches. What a wonderful way to train children to give. The work must be very pleasing to God the Father and all of us. Do not worry. Keep on and smile through it all. I am 89 years now but I act as mediator. When a check or money order comes, I put it into an account here and when a reliable person is going out, the money is sent. My eyes are not good now so I'll write no more, but know that we are united in God's Holy Spirit.

— Sister Christopher; Dublin, Ireland

The Front Side

Just as a coin, there are two sides to this program. The front side of American coins reads, "IN GOD WE TRUST." There are hundreds of thousands of African children dying from lack of mere basic resources (e.g., food, clean water, shelter and education). At that rate, the native African people will eventually cease to exist. For it is children that form the circle of life. The front side of this program shows how the American children can trust in God by contributing their mites (coins) to help feed and educate African children. It only takes 2¢ to feed each child! Now, who can say, "There is no value in a coin." Life is the greatest gift one can ever receive from another. Some may say, "Life is not a gift that a person can give to another." That's true. Physical life is a gift from God; but through people, God maintains that life. Therefore, helping others to live by providing food, clean water, shelter and even education is the most precious gift anyone can receive; and through the Children's Mite Program, children can help to appreciate and accomplish this special way of giving.

In other words, the front side of this program teaches our children not to believe directly <u>on</u> monetary value, but to believe or trust <u>in</u> the written words, "IN GOD WE TRUST." The U.S. Government may have written these words on their currency, but only by the will of God. For God's word says, "For the <u>love</u> of money is a root of all kinds of evil, for which some have strayed from the faith in their greediness, and pierced themselves through with many sorrows."[4]

Christ knew that near the end of time, our children would be swept away by the love of money. Think about it. Most crimes committed by our children are caused by the desire of money. They feel money can buy them anything including happiness, but the only result that can come from the love of money is sorrow. That is why when Christ told the rich young ruler to sell everything he had and give to the poor in order to follow him, he went away very sorrowful because he believed on money (for he had great possessions) rather than believing in God. Are you willing to sacrifice having the best in this world in order to give to the poor? If not, Christ said, "It is easier for a camel to go through the eye of a needle than for you to enter the kingdom of God."[5]

The Flip Side

The moral, ethical, virtuous and spiritual value of this program is the continual learning of God's ways—his character—in our children through giving. For the giving of "coins" from a child is one of the physical results of a caring and concerned heart. When the widow offered Jesus

---

[4] I Timothy 6:10

[5] Matthew 19:16-24

her last mite (coin), it wasn't the coin that she was offering, but a caring, humble, concerned and loving heart through giving. Therefore, the giving of coins was only a physical result of the spiritual purpose in manifesting God's attitude through the widow.

The media has caused us to turn our heads, turn off the TV channels and tune these children out of our minds and hearts. There are even those who seem to wonder, "Why would anyone leave their own country and go help someone in another country?" To them, it's not logical. First of all, America is so blessed that we do not see daily hundreds of thousands of children dying from physical poverty. The basic resources which are needed for physical survival are available to all our children. Through parents, governmental programs or charitable organizations, these resources are <u>always</u> at hand. Therefore, this country is blessed in the eyes of all nations. In America our children are daily dying from a moral, ethical, virtuous and spiritual poverty. Statistics reveals this through selfishness, violence, murder, stealing, fornication, substance abuse, suicide and many other ways. Our children are lacking a concerned, caring, and loving attitude towards life and others. These moral, ethical, virtuous and spiritual resources are needed in order to produce a better society.

Humility allows a child to be thankful for all things in life, while pride boasts about the bigger things. Humility also allows a child to be thoughtful of others, while pride teaches selfishness. Which one of these qualities would you rather see in children? By participating in this program, children will be taught that learning to care is learning to love; learning to love is learning good relationships; and good relationships produces a better

ALL WE'RE ASKING FOR IS "YOUR 2¢ WORTH."

society in which we live.[6]

The flip side of this program reveals how this whole world once was dying from poverty — spiritual poverty. In heaven, the angels praise and worship God every second. He has everything he could possibly want. He's not lacking anything and neither are those who serve him and God the Father looked down on a diseased and spiritually impoverished world full of sin with a concerned, loving, and caring attitude. He did not tune us out, but found mercy and grace in his eyesight towards a dying world.

Out of unselfishness he gave, as a sacrifice to save us from spiritual poverty, his only son Jesus Christ.[7] Jesus, our Savior was willing to leave his perfect home to serve as a sojourner. He did this out of love for you and I. So we could have a chance to be spiritually nourished in order to have eternal life in his kingdom or home. Therefore, helping others by giving, whether they be near or far, is only rendering to others as Christ has rendered to us. Let's thank God for the wisdom and understanding of His Word.

Children (and adults) often see "coins" lying outside on the ground or the floor of their homes and their immediate response is to allow the coins to remain there. The flip side of this program will tell them to collect those coins and trust God for guidance. Therefore, resulting in the preservation of humility within them in which the coin

---

[6] James 4:6

[7] John 3:16

reads, "IN GOD WE TRUST." In a nutshell, the Front Side of this program teaches faith in God while the Flip Side teaches obedience to God.[8]

Let's teach children to believe in the written words on American coins, "IN GOD WE TRUST." So that, through Christ, they can value their physical and spiritual lives. Teach them that there is nothing wrong with sacrificing their ice cream cones, lollipops, Barbie dolls and toy cars in order to give their mites (coins) to impoverished children so that they too, can have a chance to be nourished by food, clean water, shelter and education. For Jesus himself said, "Whatever you did for one of the least of these brothers of mine, you did it for me." Teach them that they will be preserving the special quality (humility) within them in which Jesus said we (adults) must become; for they are the children's mite.

---

[8] James 2:20-26

GOD'S CRAYONS OF LOVE

To "color" means "to give brightness, richness, character, worth, difference, renewal and life to an image". Children can <u>only</u> show love, care, concern, joy, peace, happiness, obedience, humility and etc. (which are God's Crayons of Love) by allowing God to color within them, by his Holy Spirit, his character; therefore, creating a new life (or image) within their heart and mind. They are learning to become Christ-like. Coloring is a very brilliant "art" which was first expressed by God, Himself!

This program is a way children (and adults) can start allowing God to use within them His crayons of love, so that they can help the less fortunate and set an example for others in caring and giving. They can help God by allowing Him to color or paint a picture of giving in their heart. Giving is one of God's crayons of love. The "coins" that they find, or sometimes are given to them by parents, friends and neighbors, can help feed the impoverished children of Africa; where it takes less than 2¢ a day to feed a child. They can also help God in coloring His beautiful picture within them by sacrificing their wants and desires and give the "coins" to the homeless and starving children of the world so that they can continue to color His beautiful picture of LOVE.

God's Steps of Love

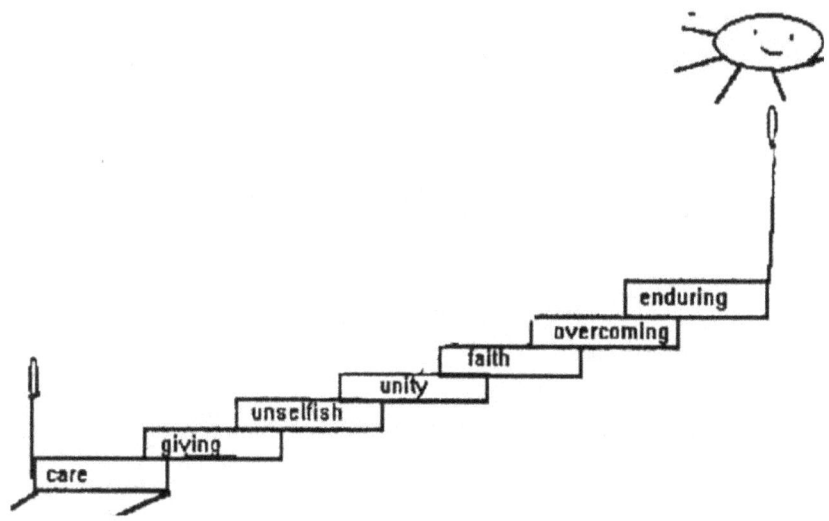

If we color a picture using one single crayon, would that make a beautiful picture? No, it would look odd and dull, wouldn't it? But if we color that same picture using several crayons, it would make a very beautiful picture. It would also be pretty to look at. Well, God feels the same way we do regarding that beautiful picture. The different colors of crayons symbolize how we are people of different races. When formed together in peace and unity through Him, we make a beautiful and pretty picture.

God wants to use us as His crayons of love, but we must first allow Him to. God describes us as clay in the hands of the potter, so why not crayons in the hands of the artist.[9] He loves each and every one of us. That is why it is important to God that we allow Him to use us as His

---

[9] Isaiah 64:8

ALL WE'RE ASKING FOR IS "YOUR 2¢ WORTH."

crayons of caring, humility, interest in others, loving, doubtless, remembrance, endurance, needing to give, serving, merciful, indifference, tolerance and emotions. God has so many crayons of love that it's impossible for us to name them all, but they all add up to LOVE. Did you know that you can find God's crayons of love throughout the Bible?[10] Those scriptures will show you examples of what Christ uses to create beautiful pictures in the heart of His children.

When we do not allow God to use us as His crayons of love; then within us, His crayons break and sometimes they even get lost. Just as if children do not take care of their physical crayons of colors, they will break and sometimes wander everywhere and never be found. That is why it is very important to God that we continue throughout our lives allowing Him to use us as His crayons of love, so that we can help those who are starving and homeless. And also those who are selfish, uncaring and unloving to find their way back into His beautiful picture; for they have within themselves allowed His crayons of love to be broken and lost.

---

[10] Galatians 5:22,23

THE CHILDREN'S MITE

The 7 Steps to Color "Love"

John 3:16 reads, "For God so loved the world, that he gave his only begotten Son, that whosoever believeth in him should not perish, but have everlasting life."

Step #1 — Care

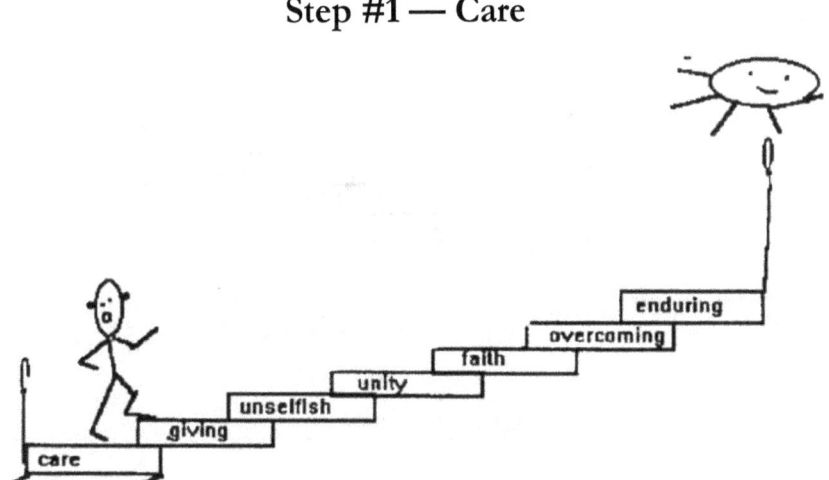

"For God so loved the world . . ."

Children (and adults) <u>must</u> walk in God's footstep of C-A-R-E in order to express love one to another. God cares and we should show our concern about the physical and spiritual poverty of others. God loves the children in the world because he cares and is concerned about them. If we do not care and show a lack of interest to one another, then how can the love of God remain in us? When we show our concern about others, then we will be <u>expressers</u> (God's light-bringers) of his love. We will be giving brightness, richness, character, worth, difference, renewal and life to a dull and gloomy world. We will be helping God to color his beautiful picture of love because the scripture states that God (through caring) loves the world.

ALL WE'RE ASKING FOR IS "YOUR 2¢ WORTH."

Step #2 — Giving

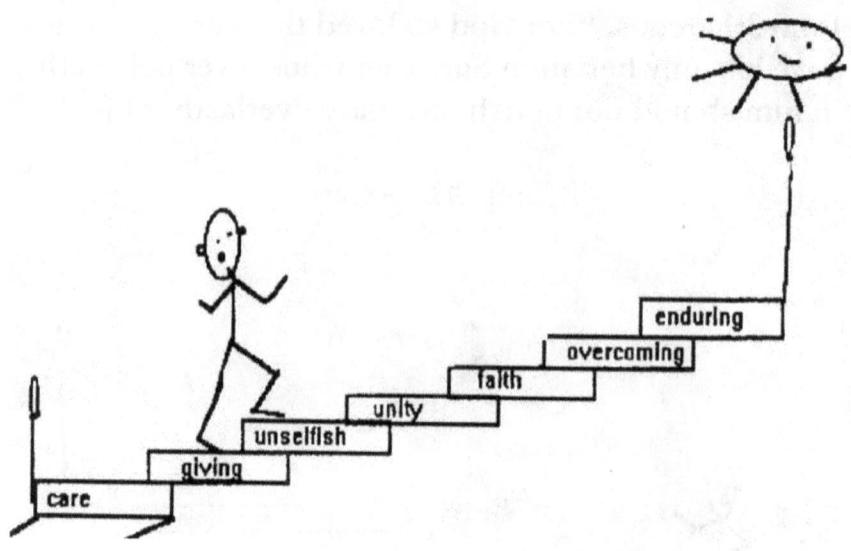

"that he gave . . ."

God is the first cheerful giver. By caring, he gave. He loved us so much and gave us what we needed in order to survive spiritually. When we see people in need, we should <u>always</u> be willing to walk in God's footstep of G-I-V-I-N-G. Giving is the sum of love. We should not dread or fear giving, but express cheerfulness in giving. Christ loves a cheerful giver (II Corinthians 9:7). Even though we gave rejection in return to God's love, he still loves us today. Regardless of how we're treated by others, Christ wants us to color (or give) a beautiful picture with love. The scripture states that God is <u>always</u> a giver of love.

Step #3 — Unselfish

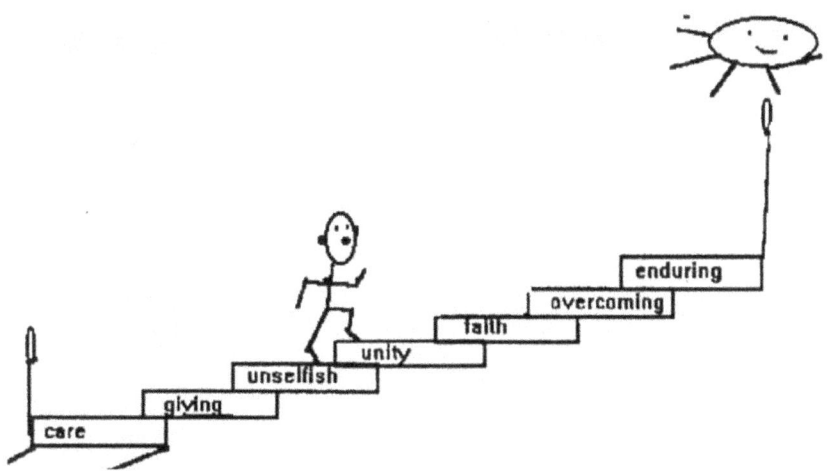

"his only begotten Son . . ."

God allowed his only son to be laughed at, lied on, betrayed, persecuted, tortured and finally killed for the sins of this world. God loved us so much that he allowed these things to happen to his only son, Jesus! He did not place his feelings above us. God is unselfish. He always cares about others and he gives us love every day. If we walk in God's step of U-N-S-E-L-F-I-S-H-N-E-S-S, we will always consider the feelings and needs of others above our own. Whatever or whoever is most dear to us cannot be compared to God's gift of sacrificing his only son, Jesus! For unselfishness is love; the kind of love that only comes from God. So let's love one another by not being selfish.

Step #4 — Unity

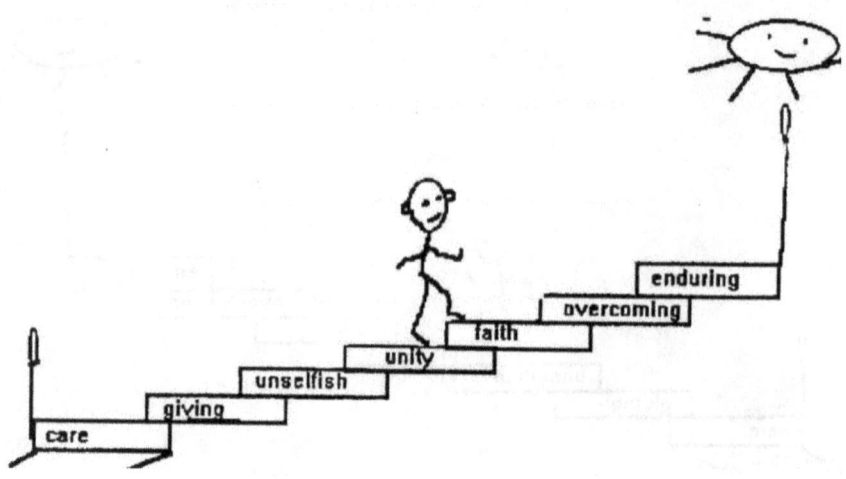

"that whosoever..."

God sacrificed his son for all of us. It does not matter what your gender, age, race or cultural background is, Jesus loves you. The Apostle Paul told the early Christians that love (or unity through Christ) was the most important part of the Christian life. He said that love was kind and considerate. Love is patient and does not anger easily or do evil to another person. Paul said that all of us need to learn how to love as Jesus loved us. If we walk in God's footstep of U-N-I-T-Y, then we will be in harmony with each other. The unity of the Spirit is the bond of peace.

Step #5 — Faith

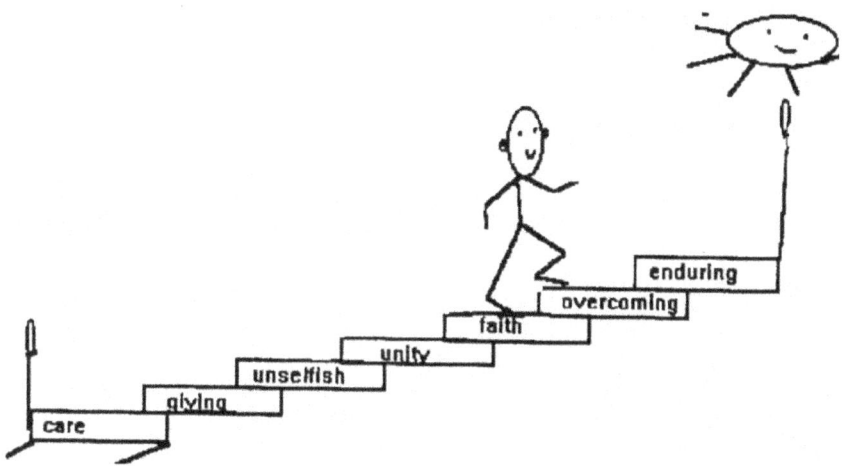

"believeth in him..."

One day a great crowd of people followed Jesus to a mountainside. They wanted to hear what he had to say because what he said made them understand more about God. Jesus told them that because they believed they were blessed in many ways. He also told them not to be discouraged when people gave them a hard time about their faith in God because believing in God was the right thing to do and that someday they would be rewarded for believing. Jesus believed his Father's purpose for his physical existence. If we walk in Jesus' footstep of F-A-I-T-H, then we will spread the message of God's soon-coming Kingdom to this dark and gloomy world. We'll be willing to become his "expressers of love" or "light-bringers".

ALL WE'RE ASKING FOR IS "YOUR 2¢ WORTH."

Step #6 — Overcoming

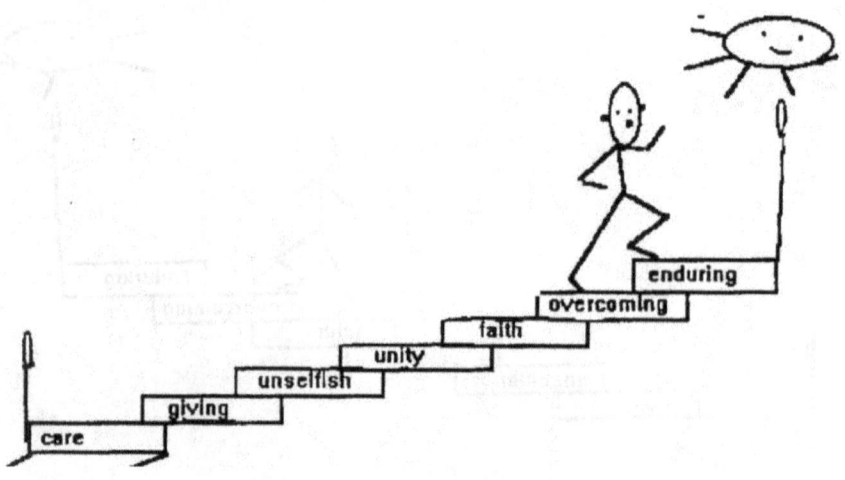

"should not perish . . ."

If we believe that God's kingdom will come, we will overcome (not perish). By believing that Jesus Christ will protect us from the invisible power of Satan, we will overcome (not perish). Satan tried to destroy Jesus at birth, but the Father protected him. Jesus believed his Father would continue to protect him from Satan until his appointed time of death. If we walk in Jesus' footstep of O-V-E-R-C-O-M-I-N-G, then we will not fear what Satan can do to us. There is no fear in love; but perfect love casts out fear, because fear involves torment and he who fears has not been made perfect in love. An example of perfect love is the Apostle Paul. He was with a group of men on an island named Malta. Paul gathered a pile of sticks and as he placed it on the fire, a snake unexpectedly crawled out and onto his hand and bit him. The men were very afraid because they thought God was punishing Paul. Paul believed that Jesus would help him to overcome or not perish by the snake and he lived.

Step #7 – Enduring

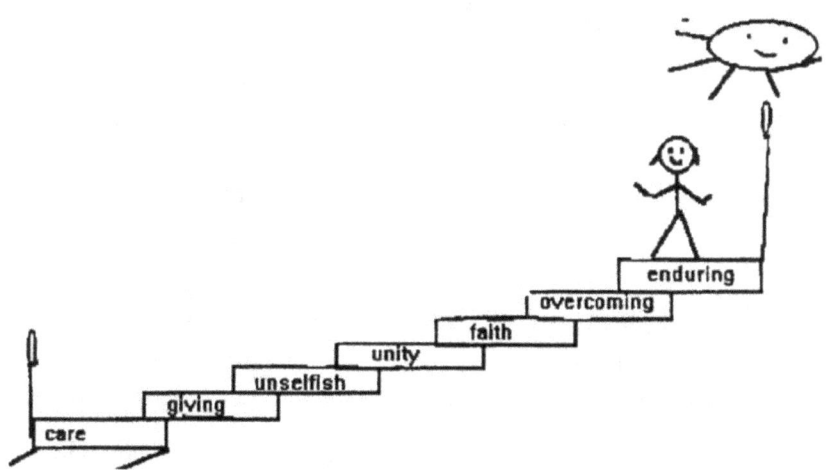

"but have everlasting life."

Jesus [1]<u>cared</u> tremendously about everyone and [2]<u>gave</u> his life [3]<u>unselfishly</u> to [4]<u>unite</u> us together in [5]<u>faith</u> in order for us to [6]<u>overcome</u> the pitfalls of this world and [7]<u>endure</u> until the end so we can live with him in his Kingdom. Jesus promised when he has endured the sufferings of the world, he would live again! During Christ three-day rest in the grave, those who loved him mourned his death. They seemed so caught up in their sorrow that they forgot about what He said. We should always remember as often as possible God's promise that if we endure until the end, great is our reward. That reward is eternal life. Endurance is patience and patience is faith. We must believe, through Christ, we will also live again!

SURRENDER TO REAP YOUR
SPIRITUAL INHERITANCE

A child <u>must</u> be trained regarding their spiritual inheritance early in life.[11] It is the responsibility of <u>every</u> adult to live respectable around them. Daily children imitate the actions of those who are near to them. Adults, ask yourselves, "What examples am I setting?" Think about it and be honest. Satan's role is to prevent everyone (young and old) from believing and accomplishing his or hers spiritual inheritance. Believe it or not!   Let me share with you my childhood experience on this subject. I love my mother very much. She would often warn me about her failures in not setting a good example for my spiritual walk in life. I respected her for that because it took humility to omit to wrongdoings. Because of the mistakes she could not correct, she warned me not to imitate her walk in life and to trust and follow Jesus for guidance; for Jesus promises to forgive and protect us from Satan—the invisible enemy.

 Children today are being encouraged to give or surrender their service to this world's government—an army that <u>only</u> fight against flesh and blood. It is very

---

[11] Proverbs 22:6, Ephesians 6:4

easy to believe and surrender to that which can be seen. It does not take faith to believe in this physical world government. It shows children the benefits they can reap from surrendering to be trained as physical soldiers. The main requirement of a soldier in this world's government is the willingness to kill others, when needed. Unknowingly, it takes hate in order to kill; but this requirement conflicts against the requirement to become soldiers in God's army of love. This battle is not against people as this world's government led us to believe, but against spiritual hosts of evil and wickedness. It's an invisible and spiritual warfare! This program will continue to remind our children of their individual spiritual battle; and by putting on the whole armor of God, they can withstand against the schemes of Satan.[12]

Children are being steered from the direction of the footsteps of Jesus, their Spiritual Squad Leader. For Jesus was never in a "payback" mode. Neither did he depend on substance abuse (e.g., drugs, alcohol or crack) as his comforter. His love was and still is for the Father and all people, regardless of one's race. It does not matter if one chooses to disbelieve, human beings <u>cannot</u> directly fight against spiritual beings—the invisible forces of evil; but indirectly, through Jesus Christ, we can!

Sharing, giving, caring, concern and love for others is <u>not</u> a part of our nature. They are the characteristics of God. Therefore, this program is only teaching children (and

---

[12] Ephesians 6:11-18

adults) to let Jesus live again within them! As Satan, under the governmental reign of Herod, tried to kill baby Jesus, he is still trying to prevent Jesus' birth within children (and adults) through denial of their spiritual warfare. Children should be taught and encouraged to willingly become trainees for their spiritual battles. For Jesus instructs them to "Be sober, be vigilant, because your adversary the devil, as a roaring lion, walketh about, seeking whom he may devour."[13]

Satan knows it's impossible for anyone to reap their spiritual inheritance being controlled by lack of self-control, hate, murder and especially racism (prejudice against the color of one's skin). If we would allow God to give us understanding on this issue, he would let us know that Satan is <u>not</u> prejudice against any human being, but his evil spirit convinces us to be.[14] Satan persuades some of us to even believe a spirit world does not exist and the <u>only</u> most Powerful and Almighty Spiritual Being that can and will destroy Satan is God, Himself!

This is why statistics reveal so much violence among our children today because they are <u>not</u> being trained to believe in surrendering their service to their spiritual battles and to believe the wonderful benefits gained from the victory of this battle through Jesus. The benefits are an everlasting spiritual existence and reign in a government ruled by Jesus Christ! But it takes faith to believe Christ's Kingdom will come!

---

[13] I Peter 5:8

[14] I John 3:15,16

THE CHILDREN'S MITE

The required credentials of a soldier in God's army of love are:

1. To believe that God's Word is true and His government exists.
$$+$$
2. To become truly sorrowful and ask God for his forgiveness of our wrongdoings.
$$=$$
3. Reception of God's mercy and grace.

<u>Note</u>: Numbers. 2 and 3 will <u>not</u> be given to Satan, the invisible ruler of this world's government. Justice does prevail![15]

If this world's government is ruled under God's reign, then why would Jesus say, "I must preach the Kingdom of God to the other cities also, because for this purpose I have been sent."[16] Jesus physical purpose in life was to preach or announce the coming Kingdom or Government of God and to teach and remind children (and adults) of their spiritual battles. Through Jesus, which is by his Holy Spirit, we are to continue to teach and remind our children of their spiritual inheritance so that they can become willing to serve as trainees in God's army of love.

We're waiting for the dramatic scenery of Christ's return. He's already here! Just as the people at Christ's <u>First Appearance</u> did not believe he was the Son of God, his

---

[15] James 2:19

[16] Luke 4:43

Second Appearance—those with Christ's Holy Spirit—are disbelieved as being the children of God. As Satan tried to stop Baby Jesus from being born into this worldly government, he is still trying to prevent God's children from being born in the grace, knowledge and final likeness of God! At Christ's Third and Final Appearance, he will awaken and call all his children (those with his Holy Spirit) to reign as citizens under his glorious government — a Kingdom where justice will finally prevail! Jesus, our squad leader, has set the perfect example. If we would follow his lead, through faith and much prayer, we will overcome.[17]

A Special Children's Activity

This play is about a little girl named Samantha. Samantha has one younger sister and one older brother. They live with their parents who love them very much. Samantha has a big problem. She bosses her sister all the time. She hates her brother because he would not spend time with her. Samantha's sister even wants to be with her, but she would not let her. Her sister would cry, but Samantha does not care. How do you think Samantha's sister feel? If Samantha treats her sister that way, do you think she would treat God the same?

Well, the story continues like this. Samantha is talking to God about her wrongdoings (or sins). She is learning what it's like to become a prayer soldier in God's army of love. The roles of the play are character expressions of how Samantha feels about God and others. Let's see if we can put ourselves in Samantha's shoes by acting out the

---

[17] I Corinthians 15:20-28

meaning of each expression. When your line comes up, act as if you're talking to God. And by the way, each word is a character expression of God or Satan.

Children (and adults), hopefully this play will show you how we might act sometimes toward God, as well as, others. You know, sometimes it is easier, through a story, to see the way we really behave. This particular story is not real, but the meaning behind the story is very real. For Jesus Christ is the greatest storyteller of them all. Jesus Christ wants all of us to love him, as well as, others; and when he returns, we can live with him for all eternity. Until he does return, always remember, we can talk to God at any time and in any place! May God continue to bless us; and children, obey your parents in the Lord.

A Prayer Soldier's Story – Have a Little Talk with Jesus

(God is asking Samantha a question about her ways.)

God: Samantha, why do you treat your sister, brother and others with hatred?

ALL WE'RE ASKING FOR IS "YOUR 2¢ WORTH."

<u>(Samantha is talking back to God.)</u>

Samantha: Lord, I do not know.

<u>(Samantha continues to talk to God through anger.)</u>

Angry: But they hate me sometimes, too. And as for my little sister, she's always in my way and wherever I go, she follows. And my brother, he does not like me so I don't like him.

<u>(God lovingly answers Samantha.)</u>

God: I understand, but don't you love me and want to follow me.

<u>(Samantha answers God peacefully.)</u>

Peace: Yes.

God: Well, you must love everybody even when you don't understand them. What am I to you, Samantha?

<u>(Samantha answers God lovingly.)</u>

Love: You are love and you love everybody even when they are bad. It does not matter if a person is a girl or boy, big or tall, young or old. You love us all.

God: That's right, Samantha. I love the bad people in the world so much that I let my own son die for them.

THE CHILDREN'S MITE

<u>(God the Son speaks.)</u>

Jesus: That's true. I agreed to become partly human so that, through me, children can love others and fight a good battle.

<u>(Satan talks to Samantha.)</u>

Satan: I hate good battles. Who have heard of such a thing? Don't believe Jesus, Samantha. There are no good battles. What could possibly be good about battles?

<u>(Jesus talks to Samantha very nicely.)</u>

Nice: Believe me, Samantha. For I am truth and the devil is the father of all lies.

<u>(Jesus continues to talk to Samantha lovingly.)</u>

Jesus: When I was on earth, I set the perfect example for fighting a good battle. A good battle is when you love someone who hates you. A good battle is when you share with someone who does not share with you. A good battle is when you are happy with someone who is angry with you. This is an example of fighting a good battle.

<u>(Jesus is the Word and the Word continues to talk to Samantha.)</u>

The Word: This good battle is spiritual. This good battle is not a war in which you kill people. This good battle is a war against my enemy, the devil. But in order to win, you must trust in me and believe I am with you always. This good battle controls how you even think about people. It deals first with your mind and thoughts; therefore, causing you to be watchful of how you think. In my written word, I warn you to do the following:

Ephesians 6th Chapter: $^{11.}$Put on the whole armor of God, that you may be able to stand against the wiles (tricks) of the devil. $^{12.}$For we do not wrestle (fight) against flesh and blood (people), but against principalities, against powers, against the rulers of the darkness of this age, against spiritual hosts of wickedness in the heavenly places (Satan and his evil followers). $^{13.}$Therefore take up the whole armor of God, that you may be able to withstand in the evil day, and having done all, to stand. $^{14.}$Stand therefore, having girded your waist with truth, having put on the breastplate of righteousness, $^{15.}$ and having shod your feet with the preparation of the gospel of peace; $^{16.}$ above all, taking the shield of faith with which you will be able to quench all the fiery darts of the wicked one. $^{17.}$And take the helmet of salvation, and the sword of the Spirit, which is the word of God;

Jesus: You see, children, always remember you have a friend in me. I am always there for you to talk to. When no one else understands; I will, but you must love one another as I love you.

Watch those bad thoughts about others! It's even bad to think bad thoughts about others and I know every thought about each of you.

<u>(Jesus continues to talk to Samantha with happiness.)</u>

Happy: When your sister, brother or another child in church tries to play with you, they are only being caring and loving toward you which is another way of sharing God's happiness one to another.

Jesus: That's correct. I am joy, peace, happiness, caring, sharing; and most of all, I am love. So, what they are trying to do is to show you how I love each and every one of you.

<u>(Jesus continues to talk to Samantha with joy.)</u>

Joy: I want to live within your heart. Please let me come in. Because if you do not let me stay within your heart, to do that which is good, then you will not be my soldier. Please play with others peacefully so that I may live within you.

<u>(Jesus talks to Samantha with happiness.)</u>

Happy: Me, too! Happiness only comes from God. Play with me as well. For I will make you happy so you can make others happy.

<u>(Satan speaks to Samantha through selfishness — not wanting her to share with others.)</u>

ALL WE'RE ASKING FOR IS "YOUR 2¢ WORTH."

Samantha: But it's hard to do that sometimes. Sometimes I just don't feel like sharing good feelings.

Selfish: That's my girl, Samantha. Let me live within you. Play with me and you do not have to share good feelings.

(Jesus continues to talk to Samantha.)

Holy Spirit: Don't listen to Satan, Samantha. You can do it. Just keep talking to me. I will help you to be loving, caring, and happy. I will help you to share with others. As my Father shared me; through me, you can learn to do those things!

Samantha: Who are you?

Holy Spirit: You know after I died on the cross for all bad people, I sent the Holy Spirit, which is my mind, thoughts, and actions to help you be good people. Through the Holy Spirit, the life I lived while on this earth can be lived again by your obedience. All you need to do is to <u>believe</u> and love God, praying always, and be willing to treat others the way you want to be treated.

(Satan continues to speak to Samantha through hatred.)

Hate: Don't listen to the Holy Spirit. It's okay to hate those who don't like you; and besides, you cannot be perfect anyway.

THE CHILDREN'S MITE

<u>(The Holy Spirit speaks to Samantha with love.)</u>

Love: No. No. No. That's not true. If you hate others, then you hate God. For God so loved the world (all people) that he gave his only begotten son that whoever believes in him should not die but have eternal life. Through me, my grace and mercy is all you need. Just believe and do as I have commanded you.

<u>(Satan continues to speak to Samantha through sadness.)</u>

Sad: But I'm so sad that Jesus had to die.

<u>(The Holy Spirit continues to speak to Samantha with joy.)</u>

Joy: Oh, no. Don't be sad. My disciple, Peter, was also sad about my death. But Peter did not understand. Sometimes things may look sad, but they are not. If I did not die for all mankind, then they would not have a chance to become a soon-to-be-born citizen in my kingdom or government. That's why you must love each other even when you don't understand.

<u>(Samantha is learning she can talk to God.)</u>

Samantha: God, please help me through my child years and my adult life. Help me to love those who do wrong to me. Help me to love my parents, sisters and brothers. Help me to spread your love, joy, peace, happiness, unselfishness and sharing ways to others; and most of all, help

me to love you. Teach me all about your
Holy Spirit so that I may understand. Help
me to always pray to you about everything.

(Jesus answers lovingly.)

Jesus: I will always love you and will be with you until the end. All you need to do from now on is talk to me because I am real.

(All the children (and adults) say, "Thank you to God for his love, mercy and grace.")

THE CHILDREN'S MITE

Fill in the blank lines in the drawing below:

The Whole Armor of God (Ephesians 6:11-17)

1. Sword of the Spirit
2. Belt of Truth
3. Gospel of Peace
4. Helmet of Salvation
5. Breastplate of Righteousness
6. Shield of Faith

Drawing by Ervin D. Toomer (1995)

CHILDREN'S STORIES

The Unselfish Family

Alpha is a loving Father whose concern is for all children. He has an only Son named Omega. Alpha and Omega have such a close relationship that they are considered to be All-in-One. One day Alpha decided that all children needed someone to show them an example of true love. He knew his only Son would be the perfect sacrifice. Omega trusted his Father's decision of love and agreed to become that perfect example. Alpha, out of unselfishness, gave his only Son as a sacrifice for all children of the world to follow while Omega, out of unselfishness, agreed.

Omega left his home of "true love" and lived among the "children of sadness." Everywhere Omega went, he saw children that were uncaring, unconcerned and unloving toward one another. As he walked among them, he would constantly remember his Father's mission—to show the need to be unselfish. Omega visited many homes. He went door to door trying to share his love. Many children would laugh, mock and say bad words at him, but he continued offering the bread of life and water of hope to the children of sadness.

Omega continued to give "true love" to the children of sadness. You see, Omega <u>always</u> remembered his Father's mission of love. Regardless of the refusals, he continued to keep in mind that mission. He never forgot and nor did he give up! He kept on giving and giving and giving love. Omega never thought about himself before others. He always thought on showing love, care and concern to the needy children of the world. The point of this story is that unselfishness starts with Alpha and ends with Omega — The First and the Last.

The True King and I

There once was a King who loved his people dearly. One day he decided to dwell among them. He stripped off his crown, his robe of wealth and all his riches. He lived among his servants as a "Master Servant" (one who specializes in serving others). As he journeyed throughout the land, he saw poverty on top of poverty. He would often weep because of the lack of concern and care his people showed toward one another. This type of poverty was worse than the poverty of physical wealth. At that moment, no one knew he was the "True King." The people treated him with disrespect. They would laugh, throw stones and curse him in return of his mercy and grace. The King had so much compassion in his heart for his people that he would <u>always</u> forgive them. According to each person's need, the King would also give many gifts. They used him in order to continue to receive further gifts. But again, out of love, he continued to give.

The King knew he had to return to his throne. He had to prepare a place for all "his friends" to live with him in his kingdom. They did not want him to leave them. They could not understand why he had to go. They thought if he returned to the "luxuries of his kingdom," he would forget them. Because of the tremendous amount of love he had for all his "friends", he promised to never forsake or forget them. They trusted him. They believed he would return to his throne and prepare them a "home of luxury" so they could be governed by his justice of love, peace and happiness! A home where "The True King and I" will live forever!

THE CHILDREN'S MITE

The Little Boy Who Colored Love

Can you imagine how Joseph felt when his brothers sold him as a slave? Joseph's parents were Jacob and Rachel. His mother died when his baby brother was born. His name was Benjamin. Jacob loved Joseph and Benjamin very much because he loved their mother. Joseph also had 10 older brothers. His older brothers would sometimes notice how their father would show a special love towards Joseph. They disliked Joseph, but Joseph loved them anyway.

Often times Joseph would see his older brothers playing games. He would join them in hopes of sharing his love. Instead they ended up tricking him. But again, he would always show love, care and concern for his brothers. You see, Joseph was a little boy who allowed God to use him as his "Crayon of Love." Regardless of how Joseph's brothers treated him, he would "color" (or give) them love in return.

Jacob noticed how Joseph would color (or give) brightness, character, worth, difference, renewal and life in any situation; and because of Joseph's outgoing concern for others, his father gave him a coat of many colors. This coat symbolized Joseph's attitude—how he <u>gives</u> brightness among difficult problems. He was known as the little boy who colored (or gave) love.

Joseph loved his coat of many colors very much! He would often sleep in it. This gift was very special to him. He always kept it close by. When his older brothers found out about it, they were jealous. They were jealous of how Joseph always colored love. So they tricked Joseph and traded him as a slave for money. They took Joseph's coat of many colors and soaked it in goat's blood. They lied to their father in allowing him to believe that Joseph was killed by a wild animal and the blood was his. Jacob grieved his death because he knew Joseph would never depart from his coat of many colors.

Even though Joseph's brothers did a terrible thing to him, he still continued to color brightness in the situation-at-hand. Joseph still cared for his brothers. He realized he could not change their attitudes about him, but he continued to color love for them. You see, Joseph wanted God to continue to use him as his "Crayon of Love."[18]

---

[18] Galatians 5:22-23

The Coins of the Rich Man

The word <u>crumb</u> means a tiny or insignificant amount, part or piece. There was a certain rich man who refused to even give the crumbs which felled from his table to a beggar named Lazarus. The rich man knew it would only take a little food and shelter to save his life. Instead, he chose to avoid Lazarus and continue to live selfishly in his life-of-plenty.

I wonder if the rich man decided to give those crumbs to his dogs instead. Who is he that has a pet and makes sure it is fed? Well, how much more valuable is a human life? Apparently the rich man could not see the value of life, whether physical or spiritual. By refusing to give in order to maintain physical life, the rich man disinherited his spiritual existence. His only concern was himself. For pride, selfishness and the lack of concern and care for others had sifted him as wheat. This story shows us how our children can either be absorbed in humility or pride. Because humility seeks to give, while pride seeks to get.

The U.S.A. is considered to be the richest of all countries in the world and coins are looked on as being mere crumbs (i.e., insignificant, worthless, useless, unnoticeable) of

ALL WE'RE ASKING FOR IS "YOUR 2¢ WORTH."

monetary value. Everyday native African children are begging for the crumbs which fall from our tables. Ask yourself, "What is the purpose for a <u>table</u>?" Well, its purpose is to be used as a tool for serving people—not to be served. If we would add the analogy of crumbs to tables, the message of allowing our children to give their American coins to the impoverished children of Africa in order to provide daily meals will be quite clear; therefore, heeding to the rich man's warning. This analogy is still valid today!

ACTS OF KINDNESS: SHOULD THEY BE REPAID? IF SO, BY WHOM?

This program will shed further understanding on the issue, "One act of kindness deserves another." From the example of Jesus Christ, it is the duty of every living soul to perform acts of kindness one to another.[19] Acts of kindness will not go unrewarded, but we shouldn't expect to be repaid by others and blessed in a certain way. God knows how and when to reward us. His blessing is <u>always</u> on time.

This reminds me of a certain story. An older woman volunteered to babysit a younger woman's children while she worked part-time. From the beginning, the younger

---

[19] Ecclesiastes 12:13

ALL WE'RE ASKING FOR IS "YOUR 2¢ WORTH."

woman knew it was strange, but out of compassion and respect she said, "Okay." The older woman's daughter would often say to the younger woman, "Mommy sure like keeping your children." She would smile, but still she felt something was strange. After a few more days, the older woman approached the younger woman and asked her, "Would you take my daughter to school every day for me?" At that time the younger woman was constantly changing her work hours and her old station wagon drank more gas than a baby would drink milk. She carefully analyzed her situation to see if she could fulfill that commitment.

Well, she lived about 25 miles from her job and the child's school. She finally replied, "I cannot see how I can fulfill this commitment because of the constant change in my work schedule. Also my car takes so much gas and if I would charge you for it, you'll think I was trying to cheat you." She knew it was very important that the older woman's daughter attended school; therefore, she needed help from someone who could stick to her commitment. The older woman replied immediately, "Well, I thought one kindness deserves another and if you won't do me a favor than I cannot keep your children." Do you think the older woman's comment was correct? Let's see what Jesus had to say about this situation in His written Word:

"Take heed that you do not do your charitable deeds before men, to be seen by them. Otherwise you have no reward from your Father in heaven. Therefore, when you do a charitable deed, do not sound a trumpet before you as the hypocrites do in the synagogues and in the streets, that they may have glory from men. Assuredly, I say to you, they have their reward. But when you do a charitable deed, do not let your left hand know what your right hand is doing,

THE CHILDREN'S MITE

that your charitable deed may be in secret; and your Father who sees in secret will Himself reward you openly."[20]

We shouldn't perform acts of kindness and expect God or others to repay us in the way we feel is best. For Jesus said: "When you give a dinner or a supper, do not ask your friends, your brothers, your relatives or your rich neighbors, lest they also invite you back and you are repaid. But when you give a feast, invite the poor, the maimed, the lame, and the blind and you will be blessed because they cannot repay you; for you shall be repaid at the resurrection of the just."[21]

As American coins reads, "IN GOD WE TRUST", we should be content with the current God-given blessings. And most of all, The Children's Mite Program often reminds us to always continue to perform acts of kindness one to another and that God's loving kindness, mercy and grace is an undeserving gift![22]

---

[20] Matthew 6:1-4

[21] Luke 14:12-14

[22] II Corinthians 8:9

IS SUICIDE "A WAY-OUT"?

 Suicide is tremendously increasing among our children today. It is considered to be their method of "A Way-Out". The front side of this program will show our children how and why to appreciate their physical existence; therefore, preventing the true value of care, concern and love toward life and others from dying. For only through Christ Jesus, our Savior and Comforter, can children (and adults) find true comfort and peace of mind.[23] The tempter (Satan) tried the suicide method on Jesus Christ when he was physically weak from hunger.

Most people do not realize what Satan truly meant when he took Jesus to the top of a mountain and told him to cast himself down. In other words, he told Jesus to jump or commit suicide.[24] He tried to take advantage of his physical weakness and use it to his advantage. He also tried to show Jesus Christ that the Father would be pleased and understanding if he did it by saying that the angels would catch him before he hit the bottom.

---

[23] Romans 8:6

[24] Matthew 4:5-7

The Word states that Satan is the father of all lies. So that means no truth can ever come from Satan or his followers.[25] Therefore, if Jesus Christ would have obeyed the words of Satan, he would have credited the Father as being a liar and at the same time, his birth would have been in vain. For the scripture also say, "For God so loved the world, that he gave his only begotten Son, that whosoever believeth in him should not perish, but have everlasting life."[26]

There was a purpose for Jesus Christ's physical existence and he did not yield to Satan's deception by believing his words. Ask yourselves, why would the Father give him a purpose in life and turn around and tell him to cast his self among the rocks (or commit suicide)? Satan knew as well as Jesus what he had to face. The weight of the whole world was upon Jesus Christ. Satan tried to show Jesus a way to avoid the pressures and trials of life which was necessary in order to accomplish his spiritual goal. Jesus was determined to obey his Father. He knew the purpose for his physical existence and he believed and trusted the Father for his "way-out".

Jesus Christ has set the perfect example for us to follow. He has also shown us that suicide is not the "way-out" as Satan lead us to believe. For everyone (young and old) have a purpose in life and we must seek Jesus Christ to show us the full potential of that purpose. He is the only one that can protect us from the father of all lies (Satan).

---

[25] John 8:44

[26] John 3:16

ALL WE'RE ASKING FOR IS "YOUR 2¢ WORTH."

If we believe and trust God for our physical existence and endure the pressures and trials of life unto our God-given end, our reward will be an everlasting existence in **the soon-coming Kingdom of God where tears will never be heard of!** Let's not make Jesus Christ's death vain by committing physical and spiritual suicide, but always remember that through Him is our only "way-out"!

AN OPEN LETTER TO GOD

The Un-adorable Child

Dear Lord:

You look down on us as "dear children". Yesterday, I held a child in my arms; a child that has been considered "un-adorable." But I thank you Lord in that what people consider as un-adorable is not un-adorable in your eyesight.

As I held this child in my arms, I thought about inward and outward beauty. I also thought about how it does not matter to you how spiritually un-adorable we are, your arms are always open to forgiveness. Not holding against us our spiritual handicaps, but through mercy and grace, you are always there to wipe the tears from our eyes. So, why can't we, as humans, love these "un-adorable" children as you love us?

ALL WE'RE ASKING FOR IS "YOUR 2¢ WORTH."

As I held this child, who has suffered much scorn because of the lack of physical beauty, in my arms, I began to understand what you consider to be "un-adorable." For the seven things that are "un-adorable" to you are not "un-adorable" to the ways of this world.

They are:

1. A proud look.
2. A lying tongue.
3. Hands that shed innocent blood.
4. A heart that devises wicked plans.
5. Feet that are swift in running to evil.
6. A false witness who speak lies.
7. One who sows discord among brethren.

(Proverbs 6:16-19)

As I continued to hold this child, you filled my heart full of outgoing love, care and concern. I saw then that beauty is not how one may look on the outside, but the very love of God from within. Therefore, this "un-adorable" child has done no wrong towards its accusers. Through you, we can learn to be caring, to be concerned, to be compassionate and to love an "un-adorable" child; because you first loved us [the "un-adorable" children of this world (John 3:16)].

As I continued to hold this child in my arms, I began to wonder how you promised to always hold, comfort and ease our hurts and pains. I began to wonder how, regardless of our spiritual ugliness, you always have compassion in your eyes for us. I began to wonder how you promised to never forsake or leave us for any reason. You are always there for us! So why can't we, as humans, love these "un-adorable" children as you love us?

As I continued to think on your mercy and grace, I began to see the beauty within this child. For that beauty was only the desire and need to be held, loved and cared for. That child began to look on me with compassion from its little eyes. That child knew that someone cared. And through caring, the child's face glowed with hope. Just like through you Lord, we have hope because we know you care. So, why can't we, as humans, love these "un-adorable" children as you love us?

When I gave the child back to its mother, the child's last expression "or choice of words" was a smile. Because the child knew someone cared. As a loving parent Lord, you promised to be with us until the end of our days. You promised to give us a home in your everlasting kingdom. Where pain, suffering, and tears will never be heard of! A home where all children will be adorable! So let's, as humans, love these "un-adorable" children as Christ loves us so that our last "choice of words" will be a smile.

Mrs. Terry B. King
Missionary/Evangelist

Dear Hearts; in 1995, the mother of this child told me how her family had nothing to do with her and the child because they both were HIV positive. Her family mocked the child and called him ugly. As she told me her story, I took the child in my arms and had this conversation with the Lord. Today, the child does not have AIDS and live a healthy life. Praise the Lord!

THE CONCLUSION

The Children's Mite is a measure of seed from the Lord. This seed was planted in the ground (or heart) of Mrs. Terry B. King in November of 1994. God gives His children seed to water and nourish so that others may benefit from their harvest. We <u>must</u> be faithful and thankful in handling the precious seed that God gives us. God does not give each person the same measure of seed. It does not matter about the quantity of the seed. God does not look at the quantity, but the willingness, thankfulness and faithfulness of heart to that which He gives; in other words, the quality.

The Children's Mite is considered to be one talent or ability from the Lord.[27] God <u>will</u> <u>not</u> give us more when we're not thankful and faithful with what He has already given us. He looks deep down in the soil or heart to see if we've done everything in our own power to profit the one talent. If so, He will exalt us. He will add more talents. In other words, He will open other doors of success. As the Word of God says, "To him who is humble, God will exalt."[28]

---

[27] Matthew 25:15
[28] Matthew 23:12

When a seed is first planted in the ground, there is no evidence of growth. But yet, by believing, you're expecting the seed to produce a harvest. The planted seed will not grow properly unless it is watered and the weeds removed on a daily basis. This procedure enables the seed to take deep root in the ground; therefore, enabling its growth. Likewise, willingness, thankfulness and faithfulness enable the seed of the Word of God to take deep root in our heart, which results in humility.

With the Word of God

We must allow the Holy Spirit to...
...water
...wash
...shower

Which enables us to...
...grow in the Lord.
...keep clean after growth.
...be anointed or smeared with the Presence of God so we can continue to grow in the perfection of our Lord and Savior Jesus Christ. [29]

Therefore, increasing faith in God. [30]

But he who had received one went and dug in the ground, and hid his lord's money.[31] Let's place emphasis on the word "hid" which means to cover, conceal, and keep secret. This unfaithful servant received the Word of God

---

[29] I John 2:5
[30] Romans 10:17
[31] Matthew 25:18

in his heart, but he refused to allow the Holy Spirit to help him grow in that which God has given him to do. He chose to hide, keep secret, conceal and cover up within his heart the Word of God. He chose to keep the Word of the Lord to himself by not telling anybody. In conclusion, he quenched the Holy Spirit.

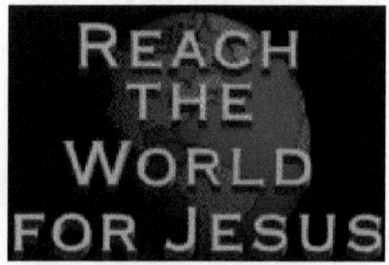

Remember, God's word is whatever He has told us to do. If God has told you to buy someone a pair of shoes, then that is God's word. If God has told you to tell someone, "I love you," then that is God's word. The Holy Bible is God's words to us. The Holy Bible is the seed of life through Christ Jesus by faith. We must love the seed or Word of God. We must be obedient and do what He has told us.

We must not be like the unfaithful and unprofitable servant and hide or keep secret the Word of God so that others cannot be blessed from the harvest. By choosing to uncover, reveal and expose The Children's Mite, a measure of seed from the Lord, many people have reaped from its harvest. They have received love, peace, joy and faith in God. One talent or measure of seed from God received with willingness, thankfulness and faithfulness through the Holy Spirit can produce a large harvest for our Lord Christ Jesus.

THE CHILDREN'S MITE

After a long time the Lord of those servants came and settled accounts with them.[32] From this verse we see that Jesus is returning! Hallelujah! He watches over His Word. We will stand before Him and give an account of the measure of seed that was given to us—to see what we did with it.

What a joyous time it will be when we hear our Lord and Savior say, "Well done, good and faithful servant; you have been faithful over a few things, I will make you ruler over many things. Enter into the joy of your Lord."

Amen (So Be It).

---

[32] Matthew 25:19

ALL WE'RE ASKING FOR IS "YOUR 2¢ WORTH."

(The End is Only the Beginning)

ABOUT THE AUTHOR

Today, Mrs. Terry B. King aka Evangelist King continues to answer the supernatural call of and by God, to do the work of an evangelist through *The Children's Mite*, a ministry of salvation, healing, deliverance and giving, with outreach ministry that includes deliverance and feeding programs, as well as healing and deliverance services. She is Founder and CEO. Gifted with a compassion for the lost and neglected, she strives to share the "Good News" of Christ Jesus with everyone she meets. Understanding the Word of the LORD God through His anointed servants, "The work I'm doing in you, no man will be able to get the glory," she continues to strive to share the "Good News" of her Risen LORD Jesus to a physical and spiritual impoverished world.

Evangelist King has also authored "Holy Ghost FIRE Talk (Volume 1)" and several e-books. Check our website for more information.

www.ingramcontent.com/pod-product-compliance
Lightning Source LLC
Chambersburg PA
CBHW051948160426
43198CB00013B/2360